Enemies of Promise

Enemies of Promise:
Publishing, Perishing, and the Eclipse of Scholarship

Lindsay Waters

PRICKLY PARADIGM PRESS
CHICAGO

Prickly Paradigm Press, LLC
5629 South University Avenue
Chicago, Il 60637

www.prickly-paradigm.com

ISBN: 0-9728196-5-7
LCCN: 2004090747

Printed in the United States of America on acid-free
paper.

Tolle, lege.

—Augustine

I don't mind your thinking slowly. I mind your
publishing faster than you can think.

—Wolfgang Pauli

What ruins young writers is overproduction; the
need for money is what causes overproduction.

—Cyril Connolly

Part I:
Barbarians at the Gates

Over the past four years, I have warned humanities scholars and publishers to prepare for a future when publishers, like myself, would go from publishing too many books to too few. Lo & behold, we have seen the cutbacks, severe in some cases, of publications in the humanities at the University of California Press, Duke University Press, Stanford University Press, and many others. Right now, the numbers of books the academic publishers produce are still at historically high numbers. This is all about to change drastically. It is a paradoxical moment that is very hard to read, just like the Last Days predicted in the Bible. Before we hit bottom, we need to figure out how to land and plan how to scramble forward.

What good are books? What are publications for? The reason I am here, suppliant before you, is my immoderate love of books, which I love nearly as much as I love people. If this be fetishism or idolatry, I am guilty. We may be—as Marshall McLuhan suggested years ago—collectively on the eve of exiting from the time when the book was central to human flourishing. We owe it to ourselves, then, to figure out what it was we most valued about the book so we can try to preserve it.

This essay is my attempt to urge academics to take steps to preserve and protect the independence of their activities, such as the writing of books and articles, as they once thought of them, before the market becomes our prison and the value of the book becomes undermined. We have entered a period of constant re-examination. As a member of our Board of Syndics recently put it, no university is going to "maintain faulty business units…simply because many university disciplines are unable to learn new tricks, or to examine what they are really about." The sky has been falling ever since I got into publishing in the late '70s. The trick now is to make sure the earth does not collapse beneath us.

I speak from the vantage point of a non-profit publisher inside the academy, who seeks to break even and also to preserve the dignity of thought and books. I speak also as a scholar. When I have delivered this essay as a lecture, some have objected: "How can you criticize the system, since you—Harvard University Press—are the system? You speak in bad faith." I say it's upon the shoulders of the insiders that the duty to speak up falls first. We publishers are not let off the hook just because of our position.

Academic publishers face dangers from all sides these days—the public, taxpayers, profs, students, librarians, colleagues. There has emerged the idea among administrators and some academic publishers themselves, who seem to feel compelled to comply with unreasonable expectations, that university presses should be turned into "profit centers" and contribute to the general budget of the university. Where did this idea come from? It's bad. We have financial records of publishing in the West since Gutenberg, and it is clear that books are a losing proposition. Widgets have been, and will always be, a surer bet. And the idea of milking the university presses—the poorest of all publishers—for cash is the equivalent of making the church mice contribute to the upkeep of the church.

I think that we scholars and publishers have allowed the moneychangers to enter the temple. We need to restrict their activities, because we cannot kick them out the way Jesus did. Of course, many universities are, in significant part, financial holding operations. Don't be shocked. So are many of our churches! Still, the universities have money that must be husbanded well, lest we squander our talents. But we have other talents—spiritual, not financial—that need cultivation. My second concern, after the corporate makeover of the university, is my conviction that, in letting the temple be turned over to the moneychangers, we have allowed those who want to hollow out and thereby desecrate our good books and publications become dominant in a number of fields, most egregiously in the humanities. I believe the commercialization of higher education has caused innovation to come to a standstill in the humanities departments of the university. The core issue may be—as Jeremy Gunawardena argues—publication: It lies at the heart of the academic process.

Humanists study books and artifacts in order to find traces of our common humanity. I argue that there is a causal connection between the corporatist demand for increased productivity and the draining of all publications of any significance other than as a number. The humanities are in a crisis now because many of the presuppositions about what counts— which is, not to be too cute about it, counting—are absolutely inimical to the humanities. When books cease being complex media and become rather objects to quantify, then it follows that all the other media that the humanities study lose value. And if humanists don't keep firmly in mind what they are about, no one else will.

The drive to mechanize the university has proven lethal for the humanities over the last three decades. The battle against the book in the West is like the assault on the statues of the Buddha at Bamayan in Central Asia, a violent gesture done in the name of supposedly higher values. We must get back to square one—by asking why anyone would want to speak, write, or publish in the first place. We need to re-orient ourselves to what it is that matters most. We need dare ask fundamental questions because much of what we love is in mortal peril.

"Cooking the Books": World War II and the Transformation of the University

By "Cooking the Books" I mean the problems of accountability that now plague American institutions: from the accounting debacles at Arthur Andersen to grade inflation at colleges and universities. This includes also the standards of judgment in academic publication. I am talking about a climate that each of us knows, in part, but that we dare not generalize about, because we know we cannot see the whole picture; yet the time has come to start connecting the dots. Our unwillingness to make fools of ourselves is the first link in the chain that holds us in bondage. We need to hazard some guesses based on incomplete evidence. My guess, then, is that the phony profits of Enron are like the false achievements of academia, represented by mountains of unloved and unread publications. As Willis Regier observes:

> In the past twenty years, the number of new books published by California, Columbia, MIT, and Princeton doubled, by Indiana and Yale tripled, by Stanford sextupled.... In 1980, Cambridge published 543 new titles and Oxford 802. In 2000, Cambridge published 2,376 new books, and Oxford 2,250.... The total output of all university presses in 2000 was 31 million books.

Entire forests are being cut down to please chief academic officers who believe they'll be raising the profile of their university by raising the "standards" for promotion and tenure! And unscrupulous, money-hungry publishers conspire in this confidence game. Modern, highly sophisticated accounting methods have been brought to bear on the work of the scholarly community and are having the unintended consequence of hollowing out the work of the academy.

Has the academic world allowed itself to be drawn into the contagious confidence game that seems to have infected much of US society? If so, our problems are more serious but harder to understand than we might have supposed. Protest against the con game in US society as a whole is growing, as evidenced in popular books such as Catherine Crier's *The Case Against Lawyers*. I'll give her some company so she does not stand alone. Crier complains that the seemingly unstoppable growth of administrative control is suffocating real work. She does not blame just the administrators; she blames the administrated: "I despise our deliberate ignorance and passive acceptance of those shackles on the American spirit." I think this sort of protest needs to be brought to the academy as well. Much is at risk in our worries about the university. I believe Andrew Delbanco was right when he wrote that in "the coming struggle for the soul of the university…there is a lot more at stake than there ever was in the glory, and sometimes goofy days of the Culture Wars."

It used to be that the heads of companies were people who knew, and took pleasure in, what they produced. Today managing the business is considered too difficult to put in the hands of the people who actually have a feel for the product. We have to have realists in charge, don't we? But, I ask, what, then, are the spires and towers and all the gothic trappings of our academic buildings supposed to suggest except that colleges and universities are places in which people are encouraged to let their scientific, philosophical, and literary fancies fly? The so-called free market—which is any thing but free—is not a concept that should be considered the ultimate framework for the free play of ideas.

The problem is that the advocates of the market say that what cannot be counted is not real. Lord Kelvin put it like this: "When you can measure what you are speaking about, and express it in numbers, you know something about it; but when you cannot express it in numbers, your knowledge of it is a meagre and unsatisfactory kind." To the extent that people consider the free market the ultimate framework, we have allowed a "one size fits all" mentality to hobble the university. One of the key figures who brought this market ideology into the academy is Nobel laureate R. H. Coase. In his lively polemic from the 1980s, "The Market for Goods and the Market for Ideas," he argued that the two needed to be seen as one and the same: "I do not believe that this distinction between the market for goods and the market for ideas is valid." This is Reaganomics for the Life of the Mind. Empiricism makes people slaves to what they can see and count. It is harder for the truth to submit to the market than for a camel to fit through the eye of a needle.

Our current problems began before Reagan and Thatcher. The American university underwent dramatic changes during World War II, because of the way the university was enlisted in the wartime exploration of the mysteries of the atom for the sake of developing weapons of mass destruction. First Columbia University, then Princeton, then Chicago, and then the University of California became drafted, or enlisted, for the war effort under the Office of Scientific Research and Development, formed in 1941. University budgets increased tremendously. And so have university bureaucracies. Since World War II the administrative side of universities has spiraled out of control. For example, as William H. McNeill writes in his memoir of the University of Chicago: "by 1944 the annual budget [of the University of Chicago] had swollen to $31 million dollars, three times the pre-war level; and of this total, $22 million came from government contracts." The perversion of the university began when universities became "captivated by the soldiers' access to hitherto unimagined resources." And government funding "compelled the university to construct a proliferating bureaucracy of its own to cope with paper generated by the granting agencies."

Money has restructured the US academy in its own image, and money is a blunt instrument. Until World War II, almost all higher educational institutions were founded in the name of religion. When some god was the name of the ultimate framework for the academy, the sky was the limit for the sorts of work that could happen in the academy, because all gods are beyond definition. I don't mean to ignore the fact that religion has often hobbled and even shackled free inquiry in the past. But when the dollar becomes the ultimate term, the sky closes in. The assumption that markets allocate resources efficiently is false, writes Nobel laureate Joseph Stiglitz: "what they really do is to generate the pressures that increase productivity." In 1973, Talcott Parsons and Gerald M. Platt warned in *The American University* that "the growing importance of the values of cognitive rationality" would harm the university because it would privilege the simplifying values of bureaucratization. The academic life is a calling, not a job. So the orientation of the academic needs to be to a world other than that dominated by the punch clock. As Stanley Cavell has written, "a transcendental element is indispensable in the motivation of a moral existence," most especially for scholars. The academy now lacks any transcendental element, and we are discovering the consequences.

The first result of the influx of money into the university was a new and much larger administrative layer piled on top of the community of scholars in departments. As in US society as a whole, the administrators became more and more alienated from their clients and reconstructed the university as "a social machine" (Paul Goodman's phrase) with a great interest in producing brand names for schools. The university was made over on the model of the American corporation, from the big three auto makers to the Hollywood studios. No wonder we have now in the universities across the country a celebrity star system run amok. Oprah seems a lot more intellectual in a genuinely inquisitive way, and no doubt is, than some of the academic stars we read about in the pages of the "Arts & Ideas" section of the Saturday *New York Times*.

Synergy—ugly cant word!—was supposed to help the university get into uniform and in step with the times during World War II and the Cold War. The problem is that the vitality of the university before this moment had often come from its being out of step with its times. This problem is a big one. Economist Peter Frumkin writes: "If nonprofit organizations [like the universities] wish to function as independent actors...they will need to take steps to protect their unique set of missions and messages." Now. Those who value the university as a place of free inquiry do not have a minute to waste.

The Growth of an Administrative Class

The shadow history of the new academic culture that was constructed to be in synch with the marketplace is made up of all those unloved books that keep appearing in sales catalogs from university presses, the same titles that never seem to leave their places in the used bookstores close to universities—monumental and inert, seemingly permanent records of the failure to communicate by the lumpenprofessoriat. The issue of the Romantic "sublime" (that is, the profound illumination that befell William Wordsworth when he lost his way hiking over the Alps) has fascinated literary scholars since World War II. In the mountains of publications that have appeared since the middle of the last century, we also have something that is sublime, in its own way—a Mont Blanc or a Monty-Pythonesque blancmange of publications upon (or in) which we have lost our way. The system of university publishing is beset with problems similar to many other valuable American forms of communication, such as the postal service (advertising), telephone (tele-marketing), and e-mail (spam). These abuses of the system make us reluctant to answer the phone, open our e-mail, or look at a new book. We clearly cannot shut down the postal and phone systems, and we cannot shut down the academic publishing system. We need to reform them. There is no way to stop the shake-up of the university press system from happening. It has already begun.

The proliferating publications are the result of an administrative desire for clarity and simplicity in the work of managing. Too many administrators prefer—just as their colleagues, the heads of elementary schools, always have—the yardstick. You know what they say: Spare the rod, spoil the professor. There may be some departmental colleagues who are incapable or afraid or simply do not want to read each other's work, but who is it that really does not want books to be cracked? Not academics, I submit, but administrators. Already back in 1962, when the present regime was taking shape, Paul Goodman wondered in his *Community of Scholars* if the university would be able to survive the weight of the new bureaucracy. Would the scholars and students be smothered? It is hazardous to single out one villain when seeking to explain what is wrong in a complex system, but I am going to go against this rule of thumb for the sake of my polemic. Later on I will complicate my explanation by describing other culprits, but for now I want to highlight the impact of what we could call the managerial revolution—as James Burnham called it back around the time Goodman was writing—on the faculties of universities. The heavies in this part of my story are the employers of corporate management techniques who have invaded the house of the intellect like the moneychangers in the temple.

Why blame administration? It is not that some leaders of universities are not trying to consider the dilemma. The December 2000 policy paper issued by 36 leading academic officers, "Principles for Emerging

Systems of Scholarly Publishing," tried to assess the problem, but they did not address the key issue of the demand from their own offices for greater and greater numbers of publications. Basically it's a dog eat dog world out there and it has only gotten worse as the universities have been let loose upon each other to fight for money in any way they can get it. They have no will to change things as long as they hope their university will end up at the top of the heap. Leading administrators, like Richard C. Atkinson of the University of California, have sought to integrate the universities they lead into the world of business as full-scale partners: Only totally unrealistic people, they say, worry about the commercialization of the university. Universities are corporations just like any corporation traded on the New York Stock Exchange, or they ought to be! Darwin and Newman were contemporaries, but for modern university life Charles Darwin can be our only guide.

How, then, to survive? I think that humanists can better their lot, and they must do it or they will lose out. There is a sense that after 9/11 administrators of universities have no patience for professors of the humanities. A colleague asked the former president of an Ivy League university if he did not see humanists playing a key role in the university at the present critical moment, and the former chief executive indicated that he expected nothing from the humanities. "They are a lost cause." This attitude is not uncommon among senior administrators who see the need to rededicate the university—especially after 9/11—to the pursuit of scientific research and money.

Stanley Fish defends the work of administrators, in an essay called "First, Kill All the Administrators," against the complaints of whining humanists by pleading that "administration is an intellectual task." His effort to elide the difference between the administrators and the administrated won't work. These two groups are at odds. There is no way around it. The MBA lot are taking over. Thus in the university we have business as usual, with a new spirit of recrimination. As I have already noted, Parsons and Platt predicted the bureaucratic mentality would wreak havoc on the universities if unchecked. In their book they only devoted one page to the emerging issue of the demand for publications, but they predicted the possibility for increasing conflict in the university between those in the academy concerned with cognitive specialization and those concerned with "the noncognitive aspects of culture."

I wonder if dismissive attitudes such as the one I cited from the former Ivy League president about the humanities are based on close-up knowledge of actual departments or sensational negative reporting on what the humanists do in the *New York Times* and (the now defunct) *Lingua franca*? For the past fifteen years or so, whenever you've seen a humanist appear in the news it's like those segments on Letterman devoted to stupid pet tricks. The tone of the articles—which the papers run year after year, just recycling them by changing the names—is: Can you believe what these crazy humanists are talking about in their annual conclaves like the MLA? The journalists then list for the amusement of the audience lectures on bizarre topics that are the twenty-first century version of inquiries into how many angels can dance on the head of a pin. Anti-intellectualism is a strong force in American life, but is it now out of control?

Universities are finding it increasingly easy to redline the humanities. Every tub on its own bottom! The rise of neoliberal doctrine has led to sentiment among the taxpayers that all social services must be privatized. Some cities have even given over their primary and secondary schools to "free enterprise." But the teaching of the humanities is hard to privatize. Literacy may be a common good, but—like so many other common goods—it has no constituency. And the taxpayers are so unhappy with the profs, because they don't like what they read about leading lights hired by major universities whose murky prose style looks and feels like landfill. Better to ditch them.

The Boom

The problem of ridiculous articles by humanists was caused partly by the vast increase of the numbers of publications that humanists (and all academics) are expected to perpetrate on paper or on one another as talks at conferences. It all sounds like a world gone wrong, but the problem is not limited to the humanities. We are experiencing a generalized crisis of judgment that results from unreasonable expectations about how many publications a scholar should publish. I am not saying there are no good publications—this is very, very far from being the case—but the goodness of the good ones is lost sight of when there is so much production that is merely competent and much that isn't. I protest for the sake of the good books that get lost in the flood of bad ones. And I am not saying the middling stuff shouldn't get published. Scholars need to write. And in fact a lot more stuff needs to come out than what is excellent because what is "excellent" often just fits today's definition of what is hot or unobjectionable.

The problem is the concentration on productivity without concern for reception. The balance between these two elements—production and reception—is gone. We need to restore the symmetry between them. The problem is basing tenure on the quantity of publications, publications few read. I am not saying that no publications get read, but many of them never do. Remember the old philosophical conundrum passed down from generation to generation by kids in school: If a tree falls in the forest and no one is around, does it make a sound? Well, the graduate school version of that question ought to run as follows: Is it a contribution to scholarship if no one reads it? For a poem, it was supposed to be enough, according to Archibald MacLeish's *Ars poetica*, for it to be, and not mean. I wonder to what degree the proliferation of unused but dangerous weapons has influenced our thinking so that all production—even that of scholarship—has come to resemble the arms race? Freud says a joke only becomes a joke when somebody other than the teller laughs. Does scholarly writing only become a contribution to scholarship when somebody else reads it and appropriates it for their own work? I think so. Why the hesitation? Because it might take decades for some scholar to read that 1894 University of Berlin dissertation in Latin by one James Henry Breasted, but when it gets read it might provoke the recovery of a lost world of Akhenaten. Scholarly effect is measured in terms of the depth, not width, of the reverberation the work sets off. Temporary celebrity is no guide at all.

The meteoric rise in scholarly publications from the 1960s to the 1990s has burst just as surely as the Dow and NASDAQ. It's now time to pause and understand just how inimical to the life of the mind this Boom has been, because teaching and serious writing had to take a backseat when publication for its own sake was glorified. But what we have gotten in many cases is only a semblance of innovation and growth, powered by hype. Throughout the university, we have been keeping the fires aglow on all the burners and the pots are a-boiling, but what's cooking? If you are a scientist, don't allow yourself to feel complacent and superior by thinking that overproduction is a problem for humanists only. As Peter A. Lawrence wrote in *Nature* in 2003, "Managers are stealing power from scientists and building an accountability culture that [here Lawrence quotes Onora O'Neill] 'aims at ever more perfect administrative control of institutional and professional life.' The result is an 'audit society' [Michael Power's memorable phrase], in which each indicator is invested with a specious accuracy and becomes an end in itself." In an interview in *Harvard University Library Notes*, Markus Meister, Professor of Molecular and Cellular Biology, laments the way scientific publications are valued with no concern for content: "Often, review committees, when asked to make decisions on appointments or promotions, will look at the journal titles on a candidate's CV in lieu of reading the papers themselves."

Reading the papers themselves! What a quaint idea! How medieval! I remember when I first heard from Jochen Schulte-Sasse that at the university in Bochum, West Germany, when a candidate for a job was under consideration the whole department would read all the candidate's writings and then debate them. No wonder European universities have not kept pace with their American rivals! I think, in fact, American universities have produced much that is new and exceedingly valuable in all the fields tilled by scholars, but we are in danger of not understanding what our true achievements have been if we allow ourselves to think that the profits gained by a false accounting are the things we ought to be proud of. We have to keep our eyes on the true prizes of academic activity—new experiments in the sciences and new experiences in the humanities.

Meister goes on to say that "in my view the biggest dependency we have as academics is on these professional publishers—especially the elite journals like *Science*, *Nature*, *Cell*—in my field—and *Neuron*. We see them as marks of excellence, as filters for excellence." As throughout all American society, what counts is the brand name, not whether the car will get you across town. And, of course, no key word is more vapid in academic-speak than "excellence," as Bill Readings has forcefully argued in *The University in Ruins*. Here's where all the bricks and mortar of the ivory tower disintegrate.

The Twilight Zone

We have entered the Twilight Zone of academic research, and now the demands for productivity are leading to the production of much more nonsense. At times like these, unscrupulous and befuddled researchers make false claims that have the semblance of more interesting but also unverifiable claims. We can see all around us the eclipse of value in a culture of over-inflation. Editors of journals, especially, are finding they don't have the time to assess because of the need to keep the assembly-line moving. But it is not just the counting that is the problem. It was all fun and games leading to the triumph of virtue over vice when Alan Sokal proved that the editors of *Social Text*, a journal that supposedly is refereed, were so eager to publish an essay that conformed to their prejudices that they would skip soliciting real reviews. That was, if I can put it this way, fraud with a conscience; but didn't Sokal's hoax expose the weaknesses of the system? What about when plain old-fashioned fraud manages to succeed and win tenure from authorities whose eyes are on the numbers, not the content? Consider the notorious articles in physics by Igor and Grichka Bogdanov in France. These people—one cannot call them scholars or scientists without soiling the terms—claimed to be exploring a fundamental question: What was the universe like at the time of the Big Bang? They produced papers that earned them doctorates because they were published in respected journals that now admit the reviews were handled without care. According to experts consulted after degrees were granted, quoted in *The Chronicle of Higher Education*, the scholarship consisted of "stringing together plausible-sounding sentences that add up to nothing."

The hysteria that has arisen about the Bogdanovs suggests that credentialing by simply counting publications is no longer a tenable process. Accountability itself is leading to disputes nearly impossible to adjudicate, like the one about the Varying Speed of Light hypothesis. This has spilled out into the public in the form of an appeal by one scholar, João Magueijo, in a popular book called *Faster Than the Speed of Light*, which lambastes the foolish and corrupt editors of the journal that would not publish his research. Things have turned ugly. The editor of the *New England Journal of Medicine*, Jerome Kassirer, was forced out in 1999 because the owners of the journal were unhappy with the ethical stand he took to protect the quality of the journal. He put quality over income. The owners wanted him to act more "entrepreneurial," which meant to stop asking where the money came from and start figuring out how to get some for his journal. He became convinced that the "enormous infusion of money has yielded financial incentives that few medical researchers can ignore." The Kassirer case makes one wonder whether "entrepreneurialism" may some day be seen as one of the principal causes of the decline of America. We have learned to not expect serious reviews of pop music from *Rolling Stone*, because that magazine does not want to offend advertisers. The possibilities for corruption are greater in the academic world, because an article for the *New England Journal of Medicine* might have to do with tenure, advertising pages, the fate of a new drug.

The system is near meltdown. But I don't think we can just walk away from the wreck. We have to ask what structural damage has been done to the system by these practices. Meister points to the trickiest problem, the problems of evaluation and judgment: "It's a sad thing to say, but we have in a way out-sourced the process of evaluating our colleagues to these elite journals." This last statement of Professor Meister echoes what I thought of as the most vexatious, not to say most speculative, assertion I made in two of my three earlier essays about how the problems in publishing bring to light even worse problems within the academy as a whole: "We got to our present pass because tenure granting came to depend too much on the decisions of university presses. To a considerable degree people in departments stopped assessing for themselves the value of a candidate as a scholar and started waiting for the presses to decide. There were certain advantages to this way of doing things. One did not need to look directly at colleagues and say that the group of us read your work and found it wanting in the following ways, so please rebut us or you must go, despite the fact that you are a wonderful person. One could say something like this: although we all know that you are a wonderful person, unfortunately the university presses of America have decided that your work is not significant for reasons they know and have no doubt shared with you; therefore, you must go."

The Root of the Problem

"Outsourcing" ought to be felt as scandalous. Outsourcing is what Ford does when it buys batteries for its new cars from Delco and tires from Firestone. What do I mean? Am I saying colleagues are too frightened to judge? Yes. Is this true everywhere? No. It is possible with deep knowledge of fields of study to actually pinpoint the academic departments across the country where colleagues are not afraid to stand in judgment. Still, most departments operate the way one of my friends says his does. "I am sorry to say it, Lindsay, but you are right in your assertion, but I feel there is nothing to be done about it, because most of my colleagues [in a department and at a university that need to remain nameless] feel incapable of judging each other's work. We feel we have to defer to you and your colleagues at the presses."

Since those articles of mine appeared in the *PMLA* and *The Chronicle of Higher Education*, many more articles have appeared, and symposia and sessions have been organized. At first, when Masao Miyoshi, Paul Bové, and I broached these issues about publishers and books being pressured by scholars to speed up the process to make granting tenure a smoother, more predictable process at a session of the MLA, we were greeted with disbelief and derision along with challenges to fistfights. I am not kidding. Few of my respondents denied what I was saying; some bitterly accused me of letting the cat out of the bag or threatening to tip over the gravy train ("thin gravy," I think to myself), but most are like this response from the distinguished scholar Arnold Rampersad at Stanford University who wrote to tell me, "Your word 'outsource' is a devastating shot about the tenure process that rings absolutely true."

But the President of the MLA for the year 2002, Stephen Greenblatt, took up the warning and turned it into a letter dated May 28, 2002, to the entire membership of the MLA to ask the professoriat to consider the crisis. Even those who rejected the idea there was a crisis in 2001 at that panel, such as Duke Provost Cathy Davidson, have now accepted the fact. The scholarly leadership of the MLA has issued the report, "Developing Recommendations on Scholarly Publishing" and it follows up on trying to figure out what the crisis is and how to address it. After the initial shock brought on by having to accept the bad news that the system was going to have to change, people have begun to roll up their sleeves and get to work.

I want to rally departments to rise up to govern themselves by pointing out how they have failed to do so but should no longer remain passive back-seat passengers. But I do not want to blame them alone. I nail the blame on the door of the post-Second World War administrative system. Listen to Dean Stanley Fish in his response to my essays: "I understand your argument against giving over tenure-judgments to university presses, but as a dean I use the process as a gate-keeping device. I trust presses and their readers more than I trust departments. I hope you are well and that the Harvard Press flourishes so I can too." This is admirably straightforward and pragmatic in a way we used to associate with the bluff honesty of Englishmen —exactly like Podsnap. In fact, many universities do not even let promotion and tenure committees look at the writings of a candidate when the time comes for a decision, insisting that they look only at letters about the work. At one major university recently, an outside member of an ad hoc committee insisted that the publications by the candidate (which he had brought with him, and thumped onto the meeting table) be brought into the discussion. After much resistance, he was granted his wish. Outsourcing is so much the norm that direct contact with a candidate's writing has been forbidden in many cases.

There is a lot to be said for university presses as the best mechanism for deciding whether a scholar's work is so good that he or she deserves tenure. Raymond Guess writes:

> It is very difficult to be judicious in judgment of the
> written work of someone one knows closely and
> with whom one works every day. In a department
> there will necessarily be personal frictions,
> antipathies, irrational sympathies, and it will be
> virtually impossible for people involved in such a
> nexus to be as clear-headed as a group of two or
> three reviewers drawn from some *other* place,
> chosen by a university press for their expertise, and
> able to report in complete anonymity. In lots of
> ways, the review process at a major press is an
> absolute model for the best one can hope to achieve
> in the humanities because a manuscript has to go

through a written evaluation by experts—to assure its scholarly quality—and then *also* pass the critical eye of various senior editors who are not experts but representatives of the general educated reading public—to ensure its "general interest."

Fish and Guess' statements raise questions: Why cannot colleagues in departments be trusted at least as much as my reviewers and faculty board? And what, truly, are university presses to publish when books have become statistics of credit on a CV and debit on a university press account? Who is to pay for the upkeep of the system Fish trusts, when presses are expected to produce tenure books no one reads or buys? Listen to this, from an article by Rick Anderson:

> According to the 2002 edition of the Survey of Academic Libraries, library purchases of print materials in general are down…and the decline is precipitous: six percent between 2000 and 2001, and roughly another eight percent in 2002. Look more specifically at sales trends for scholarly mono-graphs…and the numbers are even grimmer: according to an annual survey by the Association of American Publishers, library purchases of univer-sity press books are actually down just over twelve percent in 2002 as of June…. Look specifically at hardbound UP books, and the AAP's numbers are grimmer still: a decline of twenty percent… between June 2001 and June 2002.

According to this observer, a darker soul than Cassandra, what these numbers mean is "the printed book is dead as a research tool." Many librarians want to buy electronic gear, not books. Libraries in North America are being gouged by for-profit journal publishers. The NYU Library, for example, spends 25% of its budget on journals from Elsevier-North Holland and another 25% of it on the journals from two or three for-profit publishers who realize libraries are very unlikely to terminate a subscription. Books are being squeezed out.

So, I ask Dean Fish and the other deans and presidents and upper-echelon administrators: Why glory in the impersonality of the new system? Books—at least the ones that are actually published— have become in this system merely icons to be counted or worshipped but not looked into. We have the sales figures and they are appalling. They turn our financial officers pale and they have gradually managed to cause the blood to drain from the faces of acquisitions editors who remain employed. Flourish, indeed! How? How did we get departments filled with infantilized academics? A culture of timidity has developed in the tenured and tenurable, non-adjunct ranks. Surely the tenured are not as inured to their privileges or oblivious to the suffering of adjuncts as corporate CEOs are to their employees or stock-holders. Or are they? In any case, they are different from the untenured in having their meal tickets and health benefits paid for life, unlike most Americans. They have a lot of reasons for being conformists and not stirring up any fuss. Could it be that the privilege of the tenured—as opposed to any intellectual chal-lenges the tenured might force on the taxpayers—is the reason their clientele seem less and less enamored of them?

The Centrality of Judgment

The problem here is that the humanities at their very core—and in this they may be unlike the sciences and social sciences—are concerned with the faculty of judgment, that process in which imagination "recoils upon itself"—as Kant writes in *The Critique of Judgment*—and our souls "expand." Judgment is the foundation upon which the humanities are built. In fact, they are constituted by the process of achieving self-reflection that frees humans to perform acts of judgment, that is, to make up their own minds about how things are. Judgment is—in the words of John McDowell—"an exercise of responsible freedom." The modern humanities originated out of debates over the value of painting, architecture, sculpture, and literature in the cities of the Italian peninsula from the time of Dante onwards. Judging is a delicate activity, one in which opinion and feeling count just as much as knowledge. For example, the judgment that Sandro Botticelli's paintings merited attention was the work of artists and other persons of modern sensibility, "more passionate than accurate," as Frank Kermode has shown in *Forms of Attention*. Scholars were slow to rise to the task of assessing the value of Botticelli, but their ignorance of his work was no crime. Judgment is something that takes place in history. There is no absolute right or wrong in the matter, except the refusal to participate and the belief in absolutes. Any activity other than judging is peripheral.

So, the tenure decision epitomizes the very work of the humanities. When departments and administrators outsource judgment, they avoid the task of making up their own minds in freedom. This would not be such a loss to the academic world except that in these acts of judgment academics have a prime opportunity to generate new ideas. As McDowell has said, "acts of judging are the paradigmatic kind of occurrence in which conceptual capacities are actualized"—especially in the process of formulating judgments and then defending them to other humans.

To judge or not to judge: that is the question. What combination of the cognitive and affective senses provides me the adequate bases for a judgment? Kant made judgment, the aesthetic judgment, the center of the entire critical project, bridging the hard sciences and what we would call the social sciences and ethics. E. O. Wilson has recently proposed in *Consilience: The Unity of Knowledge* that hard science is the queen of all the arts and sciences and should now dictate the agenda for the arts, but his self-aggrandizing gesture reveals the nakedness of his imperialistic plan for domination of the academy. Perhaps Wilson is not being imperialistic, but merely opportunistic. With the humanities in retreat throughout the university, there is a power vacuum and some discipline must arise to provide, well, discipline. Literature was nice in its time, he seems to suggest, but we are beyond it now. Numbers are the language in which what is divine speaks to us. Pity he does not begin his book, *In principio erat numerus*.

Kant provides a more generous sense of how we can articulate physics, ethics, and the arts. For Kant judgment is, first of all, individual: "Being enlightened means thinking for oneself." Economists colluding with politicians might try to convince us of the possibility of trickle-down economics, but there is no such thing as trickle-down thinking. You have to do it on your own. The critical judgment circulates in a loop that includes *my* own stomach, *my* unique sense of things, or else it is nothing. Once I am convinced I have a view on the matter at hand in the judgment of an artwork, for example, I feel an impulse to share my judgment with others, and it is then that I enter what McDowell calls the "space of reasons" to use them to convince others that they will feel the same way I did about the artwork. All this thinking about judgment was once central and well known, but it has become less well known during the twentieth century as corporatist thinking emerged and triumphed in politics, business, and the academy. From Herbert Croly at the beginning of the twentieth century to Robert S. McNamara and on to Richard Rorty, leading intellects have believed that the group should eclipse the individual. Be all that you can be: join the best and the brightest and learn to love the death of the subject, your own self! One reason we in the academic world might get confused about our duty (as I see it) to make judgments is that we might believe that because of the very hierarchical world we inhabit in the academy no one really expects us or wants us to exercise our judgment even in cases like tenure decisions that seem to call upon us to judge. Another, related reason we might get confused about judging is that we might believe judging should be the special prerogative of the most intelligent among us. To think that is to give in to a confusion to which intellect is disposed, but in the matter of judging what counts is character more than intellect. Hannah Arendt wrote,

> The precondition for…judging is not a highly developed intelligence or sophistication…but rather the disposition to live together explicitly with oneself, to have intercourse with oneself.

We have to get over the widespread fear of judging that pervades our society.

This has been the great age of the corporation, not the individual. Individualism is so nineteenth century! "Don't know much about history," and proud of it. When Sam Cooke sang those words, there was irony, anger, and frustration in what he said. He was protesting how badly poor blacks were educated in the US. When our yahoo profs quote him to prove how hip they are, they reveal they have missed all this. It's just history, and history is bunk. It's past. It's over. This is the lesson New Historicists would have us learn. They laud—in Greenblatt's words, picking up the language of Joseph Schumpeter—"the ceaseless destruction of the old in the embrace of the new." In any case, even in the nineteenth century, individuality was not really wanted, except for settlers out on the American prairie. Even back then, in old Europe, Kierkegaard complained in *The Present Age*: "The abstract principle of leveling…like the biting east wind, has no personal relation to any individual but has only an abstract relationship which is the same for every one."

What I am suggesting is that it is not entirely surprising that individual faculty members began to think their own voices mattered less and less in tenure decisions than what seem like the professionally produced judgment of the university press. The university press can be counted on to deliver a professional judgment, by which they mean detached and abstracted from life. Then—so it is hoped—the individual sentiment and thought of colleagues can be almost eliminated from the process. It is also no surprise that the book becomes the trophy of professional achievement—like a Boy Scout or Girl Scout badge worn on a uniform—when the very individuality of its production and reception are no longer front and center. Leopardi has a wonderful phrase about the *sudate carte*, pages of manuscript soiled by human sweat from the hands that produced it. But our scholars want to say of their own efforts, "Look, mom, no hands!" Certainly this is more hygienic, but as a result scholarly publications have become piecework, like widgets that role down the assembly line. Production is blinkered, and so is reception of such products. Look straight ahead, not sideways. Otherwise you might get distracted from performing the job under budget and on time. Books have to have fewer ideas, so that they do not alarm the recipients of them by taxing their minds, if by chance they are read. Under this regime, everything that's solid churns into Velveeta.

The Crisis of Academic Accountability

Product is all that counts, not the reception, not the human use. This is production for its own sake and precious little else. For the academic under this regime, his or her life's work has been cordoned off from living experience; practice counts for nothing there. If we stay this course, we can achieve what Angus Fletcher calls, not economies of scale, but "bankruptcies of scale." We are hampered in studying the current situation by the fact that we do not have the numbers we need at our command. It's now time some key numbers became well known across the non-profit academic publishing industry: We have gone from selling a minimum of 1,250 books of each title in the humanities to 275 books in the past thirty years. We do not have up-to-date comprehensive figures for university presses to show the increasing numbers of publications and the decreasing numbers of income for each title, but each publisher knows with great exactness how the trends hit their houses.

The industry has changed in the following ways: Annual net sales for US university presses have gone from less than $25 million in 1963 to about $40 million in 1972 to $120 million in 1982, $350 million in 1992, and $360 million in 1994. Books, of course, have been battered at the academic libraries by the wily behavior of for-profit journal publishers who have figured out since the early '70s how to perfect techniques for taking the largest part of the dollar budget for acquisitions of North American universities. I have already mentioned the situation at NYU. In the University of California system overall library purchases have shifted dramatically. In 1980, 65% of the acquisitions budget went for books and 35% for journals; now, in 2003, it is 20% books, 80% journals. Librarians have not been protecting book budgets from rapacious commercial presses who gouge them on journals. And unfortunately the new utopian library for professional librarians is one that will be almost entirely free of paper. Right now, it is stuffed to the gills; but in the dreams of our colleagues the librarians all the clutter that books make will be cleaned away.

Many factors have caused the crisis of academic accountability that parallels the corporate misbehavior of the '80s and '90s and grade inflation at the lower echelons. Some academics have enabled publishers to produce "product" that sponges up library budgets and has won many folks tenure. We'll get the product out, but don't be too demanding. Here's where the interests of some publishers conflict with the system: The universities want to streamline the process so they can all become part of the Top Ten "Tier One," as if this were really possible. The stories I hear retold from the lips of greedy deans and provosts sound too much like the Grimm fairy tale of the fisherman and his wife. The more he gives her, the more she wants. At first it is just a bigger fish; in the end, it is to be made pope. The fisherman mindlessly goes along with the gradually escalating demands until they become utter blasphemy.

Some publishers know that the only books that really sell—or the only books they want to sell—are books with new ideas and new methods, discoveries dug up from the archive. Those publishers have no choice but to search for books that are more like one-off experiments. They are not publishing text-books or anthologies. The bias of such people has to be towards scholarly innovation and research and towards the free-play of intelligence, in other words to books and articles that look like one-off experiments. One of the things that makes the current situation intolerable for such publishers is that in these circumstances an imprint functions in precisely the opposite way it is supposed to work. In a healthy situation an imprint wins a book readers. In this situation—where publica-tion is subordinate to the tenure mill—a quality imprint means that no one needs to read the book because such an imprint means a book is of a certain meritoriousness and therefore does not need to be read. The emotional capital a publisher tries to win for his or her imprint is frustrated in our climate.

We have to face the unpleasant reality that academic institutions and the free employment of intelligence have become opposed to one another. The professionals encourage a higher education version of the same "social passing" that prevails in US primary schools. Must we acquiesce? Allan Bloom complained in *The Closing of the American Mind* that the prodigal sons and daughters and their undisciplined reading and the way they mixed low culture with high philos-ophy were bringing on the dark ages. Stanley Fish arose later to support Bloom in his questioning of the interest of literary scholars in philosophy. Surprisingly, given his basic agreement with Bloom about how dangerous philosophy can be for the young, he *praised* the closing of the American mind. What he really does is just claim closure is a fact that must be accepted: "The American mind, like any other, will always be closed." God may not—as Milton avers—love a blinkered virtue, but Dean Fish loves a blinkered mind, and so—he suggests—should our colleges and universities. At least Bloom asserted that the closing of the American mind was deplorable.

The scholarly search for the unique is different from the administrative search for "excellence." When the academy marches to the rhythms of Fordist production, it is no surprise that decision-making has become fully alienated from the grit of actuality, the "foul rag and bone shop" of individual scholars engaging with the material substance of whatever it is their discipline is meant to focus upon. And if all traces of the sticky encounter between researcher and the materials of study have been transcended, then in the final deliberations about tenure, even the humans—and not just the humanists—will have been expelled from the cognitive loop, because it will then be the case that only technical solutions are *serious* solutions to the problems faced by individuals and society. Heidegger writes, "When thinking comes to an end by slipping out of its element, it replaces this loss by procuring a validity for itself as *techne*."

It would be a fair characterization to say the academy has been marked by the development of increasingly technical language. This is the language the managerial elite of the Fordist enterprise utilize in their documents. More than twenty years ago Edward

W. Said complained that those who cloak their
thought in the obscurity of technical language—
whether of the Left or of the Right makes no difference—have turned their backs on life. This development marked, he said, "the triumph of the ethic of
professionalism." Even theory, meant to open up
things, can become the means to shut them down,
when so-called theoretical language is used as a badge
of belonging to a club and means to exclude the *polloi*.
The academic entrepreneurs (as George W. Bush
might say, to praise them) use words to separate themselves from non-professionals and turn language into
something antinatural and antihuman. Such critics
(Said again) "will go out of their way to find a technical language with no other use than to describe the
text's function."

Darkness is falling, as Alexander Pope or Bob
Dylan would write. Recently a kind-hearted Nobel-
Prize winner in economics, Robert Solow, took pity
on the humanities, and proposed in *The Chronicle of
Higher Education* to bolster them up in their hour of
need. How? What do these word and image people
lack? Numbers! "Let's quantify the humanities"! I hate
to be ungrateful, and Professor Solow is a wonderful
scholar, but I do not think his proposal is helpful.
Numbers are the poison, not the cure in this matter.

What can matter has been severely circum-
scribed. The conditions of truth have been narrowed
so that it is now recognized, as Jean-François Lyotard
wrote, that "the rules of the game are immanent in the
game, that they can only be established within the
bounds of a debate that is already scientific in nature,

and that there is no other proof that the rules are good than the consensus extended to them by experts." The managerial revolution that the politically mercurial Cold-War intellectual James Burnham prophesied, whereby bureaucrats—people who never get dirt under their fingernails—seize control of the means of production, has come to pass. It has come to the very heart of the process of judgment, and has shifted the responsibility of judgment from the mere specialist to the corporation. It has driven a stake through the heart of the academy.

Only power relations among groups of humans show up on the radar of the managerial elite, so the materials that have been of so much concern in the past—the stuff that got studied, the words that had been written in journals and books, the things we put on library shelves—fall out of the picture. It's all form and no content. This is the root problem of our ecological disaster in the university.

Is there any connection between the current doldrums of the academy and the progress and victory of the managerial revolution over the last thirty years? I think yes. One of the questions that bothers me the most is why at the present time there is so much stasis in so many disciplines in the academic world? Why has the triumph of the managerial revolution led us to such reactionary times intellectually? Thirty-five years ago, even twenty-five years ago, there was much ferment, but now there seems to be very little wind in our sails. In the next part I will show how I think the poison at the top creates poison at the heart of the university in the departments.

Part II:
From Cynicism to Iconoclasm—
The Promotion of the Status Quo

They were given the choice of becoming kings or kings' messengers. As is the way with children, they all wanted to be messengers. That is why there are only messengers, racing through the world and, since there are no kings, calling out to each other the messages that have become meaningless.
—Franz Kafka

You're a whole different person when you're scared.   —Warren Zevon

We in the academy might seem to be doing much better than fifty years ago. "Progress" is being made, seemingly, in the form of the increase in numbers of publications. Across the country I hear reports of chief academic officers eager to enforce the increasing demands for tenure, coming closer and closer to "Research-1 University" status.

This progress is but the patina over scholarly doldrums. University task forces have sprung up to find out what has gone wrong. The typical scholar feels more and more like the figure portrayed by Charlie Chaplin in the film "Modern Times," madly and insensibly working to produce. Are we in the grips of a force beyond our control? Should we give up or should we fight? What can one person do?

Is it too late to change the system? A certain despondency now prevails. How can we get a perspective on our situation? The "culture wars" of the last three decades have—I am afraid—left many academics in the position of road kill. Road kill, by definition, is flattened and thus has no perspective on its situation.

Spontaneity is essential to the operation of our conceptual capacities. Voluntary censorship has been a dominant force over the last twenty years in the university. We have developed strong inhibitions. Orwell talks in "Inside the Whale" about how difficult it was to write well in the '30s: "It is almost inconceivable that good novels should be written in such an atmosphere. Good novels are not written by orthodoxy-sniffers, nor by people who are conscience-stricken about their own unorthodoxy. Good novels are written by people who are not frightened." Only the most extraordinary assistant professor could write a good book in the present situation, with the tenure gun pressed to his or her head, and with the expectations of rising productivity, he or she is anything but free. Stanley Fish counters by saying that "there is always a gun at your head," as if we had to accept this fate. Do we?

A sea-change came upon us in the late '60s. If we allow ourselves to be nostalgic, we might remember the Free Speech Movement as a success. If we are realistic, I think we'd see the FSM as at best a Pyrrhic victory, like so many other victories of the liberals in the three decades that followed. Ronald Reagan rode to power on the back of Mario Savio. Also riding to power on the suppression of free inquiry were a number of scholars who became the architects of the regime we have lived in for thirty years, people who even now would encourage us to simply go along with the system and condemn the idea that anything new can happen in scholarship and that it would matter to the world even if it did arise.

A certain timidity pervades the academic world now. The wisdom of the day tells you: Don't ask big questions; don't ask why things are the way they are. For example, the sure way to put someone down in philosophy is to say something just like, "Oh, that Chuck Taylor, he's a Big Picture Guy." Be lowly wise: stick with the minutiae.

The New Generation Gap

The emerging crisis of the monograph—and it is still emerging, we have not seen the worst of it by any means—affords us an opportunity to ask how we got where we are, from a time when all things seemed possible to a time when only the most minimal contribution seems tolerable as long as it comes sandwiched between hard covers.

Do the elders of the scholarly community think the junior people don't understand that hyping professional responsibility is a mask for the fear of the elders? Parents always think the kids don't know what's going on, but the academic juniors (grad students, adjuncts, assistants) can see what's what. There are a growing number of junior scholars unhappy with the situation, and they are beginning to speak out. Their rage is becoming articulate. Jessica Chalmers of the University of Notre Dame organized a conference last year at Duke University. She and her crew are beginning to ask where the bodies are buried: Her conference was called "Round Table on the History and Historiography of Theory." Participant Jon Erickson, in a paper called "The Suicide of Theory," questioned the heroic account the elders give of theory and argued that all the tough, Marquis-de-Sade talk of "transgression" can no longer conceal a commitment on the part of the people who use such brave language to avoid serious intellectual engagement at all costs. Even when they talk about "negotiation," you can be sure, he says, that no debate will be allowed.

At this point the younger colleagues—whom Chalmers has designated "The Lost Generation"—cannot quite put the picture together, because they need some guidance from an older generation that refuses to extend it. There is no helping hand across the generations. The cohort of youth that came of age after the '60s group was determined—as Chalmers sees it—to distance itself from the madness of the '60s. They did not want to hear what their older brothers and sisters had been through. The '60s people did not stop talking about the wonders and horrors that befell them, and the next group did not want to hear about it, because a whole new world of ideas came alive in the '70s that eclipsed the experiences and ideas that occurred during the '60s. Graduate faculties banished all talk from "pre-theoretical times," whether that talk was by Lionel Trilling or Norman O. Brown. Those who have received Ph.D.s in the last ten years and might be teaching as assistant professors—like Chalmers—now are feeling angry at having had a lid put on so many possible topics that threaten the decorum of academically correct talk. They are furious, some of them, at being held (as Chalmers writes):

> in thrall to a process of professionalization
> A total corporate process
> Whose existence she never imagined
> While reading theories of subversion
> As a graduate student.

Chalmers feels as if her cohort suffers from a case of arrested development because the elders have refused to take on responsibility and be daring in ways that would provide inspirational examples. These rebels refuse to allow themselves to be attached to a cause, to be defined by a cause. They are now a source of grief and frustration for the group whose progress they block.

The generation issue is crucial. We have to acknowledge the conflict between generations in the academic world and the way the old seek to control the young in a way that is objectively unfair, as when senior faculty impose standards on younger colleagues for publication that they themselves did not and could not meet. In such a situation what the elders encourage is what Nietzsche called a "blindly raging industriousness" for the young. If tenure were abolished and uniform productivity requirements were imposed on all, fairness might be possible; but now we have an obviously unfair situation where people with few publications are in a position to demand from young "colleagues" achievements they never managed. Nietzsche saw this as one of the besetting vices of the modern intellectual. The only justification the aged have for doing so is that they can, which is maddening because raising the bar has nothing intrinsic to do with academic inquiry.

We have entered the Age of Incommensurability—as I tag it. The present is all that matters and the past can be swept away. The past is another planet. Figures from the past can only appear to us as our contemporaries with a mindset the same as our own. For example, in literary studies scholars now seem to have difficulty imagining that the motivations of writers they admire could be any richer, deeper, or different than those of contemporary denizens of English departments and their work anything other than "an allegory of current professional life," as Jonathan Crewe has written—in other words, grasping, short-sighted, and intensely competitive. When the past disappears, we become obscure to ourselves. We can't afford to be so any longer.

Our age—like so many before it—features an ongoing, brutal, but unacknowledged war of the old upon the young. The historian Harold R. Isaacs, who studied the generational dynamics of Mao's China, wrote that Western emphasis on Oedipus stories has blinded us (sorry about that) to the fact that if you survey history you will see "fathers' hostility toward sons (based on fear of death, displacement) is far more salient in the human story than sons' hostility toward fathers." This father hostility is "the true centerpiece of human experience." In other words, the main show is not Oedipus killing his dad, but Chronos killing his children. Patricide gives way to infanticide. And indeed there is evidence of a world-wide conspiracy of elders against the young, beginning in the late '60s when Mao, Nixon, De Gaulle, and Brezhnev realized they had a common enemy. They developed "Détente" so they could turn attention to quelling their own unruly children.

How does the war of the generations manifest itself? In two ways that overlap: censorship and defense of the status quo. In our day and age—one so committed, superficially speaking, to youth and inno-vation—both censorship and defense of the status quo have to disguise themselves. The chief thing to be looking for, I suggest, is people posing as rebels. You'll see most have no cause. If they do not have a cause, I believe, they are not really rebels. Such people may indeed be the most subtle upholders of the system. These are the people of the status quo.

A New and Hidden Form of Censorship

Censorship works in mysterious ways, like the review process for publication. Why does the rise in demands for productivity come along with a seeming prohibition upon innovation? Could what feels like the doldrums in the world of ideas be caused by the hyper-production model for publication that fosters a form of censorship and a shying away from the power of ideas to disrupt routine? By slowing down the machinery of scholarly production and looking at it closely, I think we can begin to ask how it was that the content of academic work and judgment got downgraded and nearly disappeared as the most critical element in the process.

I know from my own work that the most important and delicate part of publishing is the reviewing of manuscripts. The limits of what any single editor can know makes editors subject to manipulation. In my first months on the job, I found scholars trying to use me—if I would just be a cipher—to strengthen their own causes, such as the venerably ancient one of achieving revenge on their enemies (you know what I mean—the monks at one another's throats, or, more likely, backs). Many hope to bribe people in my position with favors. "I'll throw you the chance to publish this distinguished lecture series if you'll just agree to publish my own book first." Every human motive comes to the fore cleverly and not so cleverly disguised by those who struggle in these small arenas. With hindsight, I can see how people try to play me, and sometimes, despite my vigilance, I get played. It's an occupational hazard. I am interested in other matters.

Scholars are finally expressing an interest in the history of peer review. Peer review began in the sixteenth and seventeenth centuries and took at least two forms. The early printers had on staff "correctors" who vetted manuscripts while typesetting, and who helped authors revise. The better presses became better by having correctors who helped authors make their books more authoritative. The leading researcher into peer review (other than Anthony Grafton) as it developed in the field of science in the early modern era is Mario Biagioli, who has suggested that the way we review books and articles these days encourages caution and self-censorship in much the way it did in early modern Europe. Productivity may be up, measured in sheer output of pages of scholarly writing, but innovation is down. In his essay, "From Book Censorship to Academic Peer Review," Biagioli shows—by looking at seventeenth-century academies in Europe—how the process of peer review emerged out of the mechanisms for book censorship and quickly became caught up in the production of academic value. But the most disturbing question Biagioli poses is whether or not peer review is once again in the business of censorship?

And so one has to try to get outside the dominant paradigms of the moment to find good projects and give them good reviews. It is possible to do this, but it takes a lot of effort. On the rare occasion, a project is so provocative that it elicits a review that manages to dramatize the pros and cons of publishing the book for our faculty board. Roy Porter's letter to me evaluating Bruno Latour's *Science in Action* for the Syndics of the Harvard University Press began this way:

> Imagine yourself as a publisher in 1759 confronted with the ms of Voltaire's *Candide*. Do you take the risk, or risk missing out on something which will create a vast buzz of excitement? I fear you are somewhat in this position, for Latour's book has an exceedingly Voltairian stamp to it. On the plus side…On the other hand…

The report went on for three pages single-spaced. Something about the rhetorical play of the manuscript under review made the reviewer feel that if he conveyed the intellectual playfulness and seriousness of the project, a Board of Syndics would approve it. He was right, but with a less engaged and a more narrow-minded board, he might have been wrong. It is in the fight to make the case for such books that I am really doing my job for scholarship. It is there—where Latour was exploring—at the margins of what is know-able that things get really interesting and murky. But if you do not, as an editor, do this, the drive to censor the unusual will triumph. You, too, can become a broom of the system. This is not the heavy-handed censorship we might expect in Oceania. This isn't even McCarthyism, but it is still very harmful, because it puts restrictions on what gets counted as scholarship and it also seeks to stop people from pursuing certain lines of inquiry. It is censorship that limits what can be talked about by saying that what counts as scholarship is what matches up with the status quo.

How is this sense of obligation instilled in young humanists? The way censorship operates is not really so hidden. The general talk of the age in the university makes the defense of the status quo so unpalatable that people who feel inclined to defend it have to disguise themselves as innovators and not the enemies of promise they really are. But let us not pretend any longer that everyone is interested in the free development of ideas and scholarship. Let us not pretend any longer that academics are intellectuals. The talk about public intellectuals that was so hot in the '90s was confusing, and especially to those in the academy whom it flattered by making them think themselves very important. Very, very few academics are intellectuals any more, let alone public intellectuals like Daniel Bell or Mary McCarthy.

The academy and the free use of intelligence are too often locked, not arm in arm, but in mortal combat. There's something about an institution that loves walls. There is in fact a sort of collusion—I should call it "synergy," shouldn't I?—operating between a managerial system that doesn't want to be bothered with the details of innovation or content, and those within the departments at universities who are the enemies of innovation. But it's not synergy productive of life, but rather cynicism, a cynicism unto death.

Do I exaggerate? Contemporary society pays lip service to the innovator, but really loves the conformist. Hannah Arendt wrote of America that its:

society expects from each of its members a certain kind of behavior, imposing innumerable and various rules, all of which tend to 'normalize' its members, to make them behave, to exclude spontaneous action or outstanding achievement.

But even 170 years ago, Tocqueville noted how uncritical many Americans can be of their own behavior. Kierkegaard at the same time noted the same lack of self-criticism among the learned of Denmark: "More and more individuals, owing to their bloodless indolence, will aspire to be nothing at all—in order to become the public." In 1952, Solomon Asch wrote the classic study about the overwhelming tendency of individuals to go along with the judgment of the group, even when they know doing so is wrong.

Things have not changed much in this regard since then. The '60s made all of us feel like rebels, but it ain't so. It is sad that a highly informed people can be so lacking in the desire to think things through, even for themselves as individuals. I call it the Lake-Woebegone Syndrome: Since we all know we are all above average, let's just leave it at that. I'm OK, you're OK. Judge not, lest ye be judged. Here is where the reluctance and refusal to judge hollow out the enterprise. My guess is that what we think goes like this: All of us lucky enough to be inside this system know we've been dealt good hands; so we have decided to just hold on to our cards and not play. As Dylan sang in 1997: "Some trains don't carry no

gamblers, no midnight ramblers like they did before."
The times they done a-changed back to the way they
was before.

Another way to put it: We've agreed to be part
of a collective perception. Boomers listened to those
Stones songs over and over, but that was a long time
ago, and we don't hear about them old midnight
ramblers no more. And ever since gambling became
legal, people don't gamble at anything else in life.
This regime has the advantage that no one loses. At
least that's the way it's supposed to seem. The reason
we don't walk away or complain is fear, fear of
ridicule, fear we'll miss out on something. This is the
time of the Last Men, cynical beings who—as Frances
Fukuyama says—put "self-preservation first of all
things." They actually have no idea that tomorrow will
ever come and that their grandchildren will have
somehow to manage to flourish in the world they have
made.

It is as if the Last Men do not really believe
what they say when they say that ideas have no consequences and new ideas will never arise. And so the
Last Men patrol departments of English to ferret out
new ideas and kill them before they catch on. By their
fruit ye shall judge some; by their blight ye shall judge
others. As Emerson wrote long ago, "The virtue most
in request in society is conformity. Self-reliance is its
aversion." More deathly than peer review is peer pressure. "You won't get credit for such a publication
when it comes time for a promotion or a raise." And,
"You'd better not attack the ideas of this senior
member of the profession in print, you lowly assistant

professor, if you know what is good for you." These are the sorts of statements that I hear about more and more from junior professors, and such statements, coming from department chairs as they do in both cases, serve as strong disincentives to pursue unusual lines of inquiry. There is much censorship before projects ever reach the desks of editors.

The Problem:
Timidity Masked as Boldness

The problem is that issues never get broached because they have been ruled out of bounds. This is, no doubt, a perennial problem in the academic world, which is why people in Europe have had low expectations for innovation from universities. But—as my friends in China remind me—the US is a young country and its scholarly traditions are not well-rooted yet. The way the society of the US is structured, the university is the main home for the intellect. We have no Grub Street. It is basically impossible to get along in America as a free-lance journalist.

So the university has come to be one of the key seedbeds for innovation. America faces a special problem now if intellectual innovation continues to be suffocated in our universities, as part of the overall neoliberal agenda to squeeze out all the waste in society. Censorship has become pervasive in our society but it is very hard to pin down, very hard to understand how it spreads. The "conservatives" have become radical revolutionaries, but they don't brandish Mao's little red book but take pride in hardly reading at all, that is, take pride in books little-read, as President Bush does. Many books, hardly read at all. And so the ability of scholars to innovate becomes undermined.

The time we live in is like the Last Days promised in the Bible in which it would become very hard to tell up from down. And so we have prominent

scholars who rule out troubling issues with a certain
kind of boldness, but that boldness—I argue—masks
timidity. The scholars who at the present moment
pose as our boldest contemporaries gathered together
at the University of Chicago to denounce the stupid
hopes they'd held when younger that any new ideas
that they might develop could change the nature of
scholarship. They did not sound like the one-time
revolutionaries who recanted at the Moscow Trials.
No, they did not hang their heads in shame. Rather,
they crowed their apostasy. Irving Kristol is the model
for Stanley Fish and not Trotsky. He was a loser. They
intend to be winners.

 The abandonment of critical inquiry and the
renunciation of bold hopes for innovation are
presented as themselves the very cutting edge of innovation. This is why the present moment in scholarship
is hard to understand for what it is. But if we attend to
details we can see, I suggest, how this boldness justi-
fies abandoning what I would call the Hippocratic
Oath for humanists, which demands that humanistic
scholars not pass by ideas or evidence that contradicts
their theories but face them just as a doctor can leave
no sick person untreated. Let me be specific. Richard
Rorty has argued for simply bypassing the problematic
philosophical notion of "consciousness" which has
been one of the most puzzling ideas in philosophy
ever since Descartes. Words like "consciousness,"
"experience," and "truth" have become sources of
acute embarrassment for most humanists in the course
of the last thirty years. John McDowell comments that
sweeping aside words and ideas one does not want to

consider seems "amazingly bold. But from another angle, there is timidity in the Rortyan posture of avoiding vocabulary, as compared with making the admittedly dangerous tools safe for use. Timidity is not something to be proud of."

Boldness, even bullying, is accompanied by a certain unctuous timidity when academics are the perpetrators. As McDowell argues, academics like Rorty are given to grandly ruling out what might seem to many other thinkers highly relevant issues, such as the issue of "consciousness" in modern philosophy. The academy has become, I am afraid, too much like the "real world." The profs are no longer a breed apart—mendicants, ascetics, people oriented towards other worlds. They are crafty and slippery characters. And so we see in the academic realm as unedifying a spectacle as what we witnessed in politics when a set of Republican lawmakers pilloried Bill Clinton for his lack of respect for his wedding vows only to be revealed—a number of them—as men who had strayed from the straight and narrow into the arms of women other than their wives. Beware false prophets; beware even of what I tell you.

Against such trickery, I assert the value of a return to what Nietzsche called philology, that is, a deference to the words that are actually on the page from which the interpreter has bounded off to his own conclusions. The same feeling might overcome the readers of scholarly writing like that of Stanley Fish on Milton's *Areopagitica*, an interpretation that moves beyond what might be called a cynical manipulation of the object of humanistic inquiry to desecration of the sacred books of the field of literary studies. In other words, iconoclasm. In *How Milton Works*, a book written explicitly to make all future scholarship on Milton seem unnecessary, because Fish claims to have taken up every single issue that might ever occur to readers and scholars and thus to have made it possible for Milton scholarship to come to an end, Fish devotes a chapter to the work of Milton considered by readers over the centuries to be the greatest argument against censorship and for freedom of publication and a tribute to the power of books to change people's lives. Milton wrote: "Books are not absolutely dead things, but doe containe a potencie of life in them to be as active as that soule was whose progeny they are; nay, they do preserve as in a viol the purest efficacy and extraction of that living intellect that bred them." So said Milton. Wrong on all counts, says Fish. What interests me is the boldness of the move with which Fish rules out what generations of readers have considered Milton's central tractate. At the beginning of his consideration of *Areopagitica* Fish quotes the hallowed lines of Milton—which deliver the equivalent of the Gettysburg Address on behalf of books— and he rejects their relevance to an understanding of what Milton is saying. What moved Lincoln were dead bodies; what moved Milton were dead letters. Both found the dead quick with life. But Fish declares the statement of Milton "unMiltonic" and sweeps them into the dustbin of history. This sounds bold, breathtaking. We all love to hear and read lines like that. As Philip Larkin said, we love to hear people seem to take such audacious, purifying, elemental moves. They have the ring of that line in the movies, "Take that, you bastard." But I think such boldness masks timidity, because a consideration of the rejected paragraphs would have created insuperable problems for the interpretation the scholar wants to impose on the treatise of Milton. One gasps in shock as one reads the scholar's words, but then what does one do, acquiesce? And what if the bastard who is getting it between the eyes is John Milton? In fact, Milton scholars in North America have acquiesced in the face of such chutzpah; and so timidity begets more timidity in the wake of the authoritative gesture. What did Milton do to earn this manhandling? The problem, I think, is that he locates a source of value for humans in an object. Our postmodern humanist cannot stand being deferential to a mere thing.

Here I think postmodern cynicism morphs into iconoclasm, or "biblioclasm." Philology and deference to the actual words of the writer are swept aside. If Foucault proclaimed the death of the author, Fish represents the death of the book. Like a radical protestant in seventeenth-century England Fish believes human interest in anything outside his own soul is idolatry, therefore it is imperative upon all good Christians to smash idols. Strange bedfellows, Foucault and Fish, you might say? For Fish procedure and coercion go together like horse and carriage. Foucault during part of his career saw resistance as merely an effect of power. Reason is force. To discipline is to punish. When Foucault and Fish are mixed, as they were throughout the '80s and '90s on reading lists and in course-packs, they make for a lethal cocktail that is a fully elaborated theory of why conformism became so catching as a style of behavior. That spirit of conformism gave the scholarly productions of the time the air of claustrophobia.

And so it came to be believed by many that the book is dead as a thing whose own content and form might not conform to the will of the masterful reader. This bullying attitude to the text poses a deadly threat to the book just as do the number-crunching administrators or the librarians who want to clean their shelves of printed material. In other places Fish has urged students not to read any more books than they have already read, because they are "already in possession" of anything they will ever need to know. He isn't totally committed to the system of adding more and more publications for this reason: no book makes a difference. This attitude of indifference to the content of books seems to be a fundamental belief of the new managers of the university. "Few things have contributed so greatly to dehumanization," writes Adorno in *Prisms*, "as has the universal human belief that products of the mind are justified only in so far as they exist for men." Books, for Fish, are "a thing indifferent"; and he claims Milton believes the same thing. Perhaps we are to have the dubious honor—that Milton's Loyalist detractors never had—of getting rid of him? Will we wake up from our nightmare one day, dreaming we see Milton alive as you or me accusing us of having put him to death?

This is scholarship written in the spirit of the "Last Men" as Francis Fukuyama has analyzed that type. And so we have littered around us the decay of literary works now turned, thanks to such scholarship, into colossal wrecks. And, indeed, we do have a sense now in literary scholarship that we are living in the time of scholars who have come to end things, to write the last book on Jane Austen or any other writer's work so that after the appearance of the scholarly work of the Last Man all newcomers would have to give up. The motto over the door of this academy would best be *Lasciate ogni speranza voi ch'entrate* [Renounce all hope you who enter]. No wonder the young who aspire to scholarly careers are playing it safe or abandoning ship.

Here we come to the heart of the problem Catherine Crier talked about in her analysis of what ails the US in the wake of the managerial revolution. She said her problem was more with the administered than the administrators. Too many people in this country like to be managed, and academics are fools if they think they are exempt from this pervasive attitude, the climate of our lives. They are certain they would never acquiesce to authoritarian forces the way Rush Limbaugh's "dittoheads" do. But this is not true. Now, if you want to talk about ideas with consequences, theory with teeth, consider the effects of the political theory of Leo Strauss, Alexandre Kojève, and Allan Bloom. All of them are central to the ideology of the ruling party in the US. And central to Kojève is the idea that Hegel's theory of the master/slave relation explains a great deal in modern society. When we acquiesce in the distortions of philological fact the way Rorty and Fish ask us to do, we become slaves.

Nothing is more harmful to the life of the mind than such self-imposed blindness.

What we have seen increasingly over the last thirty years in the humanities is the triumph of the "Don't Go There" Doctrine. Rorty rules "consciousness" or "truth" out of consideration; for Fish it is the very words Milton employs or literary theory and philosophy. But this doctrine breaks the Hippocratic Oath, which says, "You Must Go There," exactly where you don't want to go. Just as the doctor has no choice but to attend to the ailing person, so the humanist has no choice but to attend to that which threatens his theory. Claiming you reject all theorizing as a matter of principle is not an acceptable alibi.

And so a narrow-minded professionalism rules the roost, because the God of Small Minds loves a blinkered intelligence that flatters itself in its timidity about dangerous ideas by telling itself that ideas have no consequences. It all adds up to a defense of the status quo. You have to grant the captains of academic industry this: They do not conceal their animosity to ideas, to the foreign, to the new, to change. How—you might ask—could a scholar be opposed to ideas? Fish has argued just recently that since philosophy deals with generalities and literature with particulars, by definition the two fields can have nothing to do with one another. "You can't get from one to the other," he says. But having theories is the condition of our knowing things. It's as basic as that. Quine writes: "I see all objects as theoretical…Even our primordial objects, bodies, are already theoretical." Wordsworth thought the same.

The Slide into Negativism

These last few decades (since the death of Martin Luther King, Jr., since the oil crisis, since Reaganomics, since Thatcher) have thrown the humanities into a mood of unshakeable despondency and negativism. In literary studies much of this negativism has been focused upon attacking theory. In a long series of essays Stanley Fish, for example, has sought to kill—and even claims to have slain— "Theory Hope."

Here I would refer you to Fish's essay, "Consequences." Those opposed to new ideas, like Fish, defined the quest for them in a way they suited their own will to power, but not the way most theorists would understand what they are doing. Because they want to characterize theory as an impossible project, what they talk about as theory has nothing in common with the Kantian idea that theory is what emerges when our ways of constructing the world crash up against the world. Fish, puffed up like Dirty Harry or the Terminator, builds a straw-man version of theory and burns it on a bonfire. If this debate had been conducted by my high school debating club, this would all have been really amusing. But we are not talking about high school, and this situation is definitely not amusing. Theory, despite what Fish says, exists at the border between mind and world, and that shoreline constantly shifts. The hope for theory is the hope that something new will come into view and that we will find the words to describe it. To choose theory is to choose life over and against death. Fish crows that his little deconstruction operation has demolished theory. He claims that after his expert demolition, it should be apparent to all that "now theory has been deprived of any consequentiality whatsoever and stands revealed as the helpless plaything" it really is. But all he has revealed is the workings of the will to power clearly unconcerned with the goal of understanding. Fine for the courtroom or the basketball court, but not for the university.

I think that what Fish has really sought to slay is not just theory but the academic youth who explore it and who hope that theory or anything else we might consider *as if for the first time* could make the slightest bit of difference. He is not so much opposed to theory as consequentiality itself, the idea that *anything* could make a difference in our lives. Here a kind of fundamentalist religion morphs into cynical sophistry, as happens so often in the American marketplace where the preacher and the snake-oil merchant share the same platform, even the same body. It is just this sort of alliance that produces the chemistry that is necessary to dissolve, or hollow out and undermine, the humanities.

The war against the young and the new might take as its motto the line "be lowly wise." Attempts to match or evade the gods of the profession are doomed. So it is claimed. The energies people feel when they are young are wonderful but they need to be dispelled, because even though they are protean, they are illusory. If the young find Fish and his ilk dispiriting (and believe me, some do) it is no mistake, and it is what such "experienced" professionals mean to convey to them—for their own good, so they'd claim. One young man wrote, in 1913:

> More and more we are assailed by the feeling: our youth is but a brief night...[which] will be followed by grand "experience," the years of compromise, impoverishment of ideas, and lack of energy. Such is life. That is what the adults tell us, and that is what they experienced.... The philistine has his own "experience"; it is the eternal one of spiritlessness.

That young man was Walter Benjamin. Another young man wrote, in 1965,

> They say sing while you slave
> and I just get bored.

That was Bob Dylan.

Both Fish and Rorty represent a major trend towards negativism within the academy over the last thirty years, and their anti-theory position marks them so more than anything else. The idea that now pervades the academy is to avoid ideas. The most devastating put-down we have is that someone is a "Big Picture" thinker. Big ideas and grand narratives of liberation—those are all passé now. Andrew Abbott writes, "Theory and methods have very little to do with each other in the discipline [of sociology] today." And this is the field of Max Weber, Theodor Adorno, and Talcott Parsons!

The key is reducing the role of the individual to nothing. Our ruling orthodoxy calls for the systematic eradication of the individual, whether scholar or civilian. Fish is explicit about the rejection of the individual (as is Rorty). Fish explains the pedagogy he urges upon us thus: "Students are trained first to recognize and then to 'discount' whatever was unique and personal in their response [to artworks] so that there would be nothing between them and the exertion of the text's control."

My real concern is what is the effect of such behavior upon the young? I can see that the effect on the aged and aging has been destructive, but what effect upon future generations? One way of understanding our predicament is to say that what a Fish or a Rorty does is to make the case that there will be no paradigm shifts. There will be no times of revolutionary science. What they seem to be saying is really more soul-destroying than that, because what they are saying is that, if any of you by any chance ever think you have a glimpse of some idea or fact that is new, you are kidding yourself and you need to squelch any such impulse. These Last Men want to kill off subjects, not open them up, to have the last word, not the first. They "would rather be present for the funeral than the birth," in the words of Greil Marcus. As satirist Frederick Crews says of such people, they believe the job of humanists is just to keep cranking out insignificant publications "so that the presses can keep humming and we can all (well, most of us) retain our jobs and keep making the conference rounds." Don't concern yourself with big issues, theoretical issues, issues that cause you to peak over the fence of your discipline. No. Think small. As Derrida might have said: *Il n'y a pas de hors-boîte.* "Learn but to trifle," as Pope has one of his characters put it in *The Dunciad*.

The modern university takes the present organization of knowledge into separate disciplines, all those gated communities, as inevitable and as natural as the categories of niche-marketing. The blinkered professional who has become the norm is not an intellectual who reads promiscuously in the hope he or she might come upon a book that will change his or her life. In his or her reading and writing, this modern scholar knows it is best—as publisher William Germano advised book writers in an essay for *The Chronicle of Higher Education*—to "think inside the box." Curb your enthusiasm! Fifty years ago, even as recently as thirty years ago, scholars thought it a virtue to be widely read outside one's own field. Not any more. A lot of the innovation that took place then occurred because people tried out the ideas from a field other than their own. They made mistakes, of course, but there was then a tolerance for experimentation that is unacceptable in our more professionalized era. Now we accept the idea that each field is separate and that the professional has little to gain by intellectual promiscuity.

These last thirty years have indeed been our Babylonian Captivity, but it is time to escape it. Fish has proclaimed again and again that all of us in literary studies are part of a system that prescribes in advance what we can know and think. The way of life of the professional is its own justification, says Fish: "The pressure of professional life leads to the proliferation of work (research projects, publications, etc.) that has no justification in anything but the artificial demands of an empty and self-serving careerism." What's your problem with that? Would you like professors of literature to read outside their field? Nice, but not essential, and probably even detrimental to their careers. In fact, it seems that nothing is more reprehensible in a good academic to Fish and his progeny than curiosity, following will' o' the wisps, chasing ghosts. Kills cats; will kill you. Will certainly cause you not to get tenure. Good professionalism is marked by a blinkered and cloistered virtue. If you think the academic should be an intellectual, you are just plain mistaken. The good academic hunkers down in one limited domain and pays no attention to what else is going on in the realm of ideas and the arts. Fish: "It is perfectly possible for someone wholly ignorant of [other fields] to operate quite successfully in [his or her own field.]" The young who hope that learning some new theory or reading some new book will spark some new thought are wrong, wrong, wrong again. Theory can have no consequences because any question that can arise within literary studies has already been imagined by our predecessors. Fish again: "Theory is an impossible project which will never succeed."

Why, Despite All, Books Still Matter

Call me an idolater, then. I believe that books can change us, that they have in them, the best of them, the ability to interact with us in ways that bring new things to life. But we have to let them affect us. Words and books for our pragmatists are putty—malleable things to use for the greater purpose of dominating people. The goal is the triumph of the will over all. The greatest theorist of reading in the twentieth century was Marcel Proust, whose idea about how close reading triggers the activity of our involuntary memory inspired the criticism of Walter Benjamin, Paul de Man, and Edward Said, among others. For pragmatists critical readings offer opportunities to assert one's will over texts and humans, but Proust encourages a reading that proceeds without human will dominating. Against our pragmatists with their conviction that nothing new can or will arise within university research, I call up the ancient Christian humanist, Augustine, whose mantra was *Tolle, lege*: take up and read the book. Augustine counters our contemporaries who hollow out the book of any significance or content, because Augustine believes an object, a book or a movie or a song, some artifact outside my body, could draw me into an interaction that would change my soul. The sad truth, however, is that way too many profs now believe artworks can best be used as the means to teach morals—they can be like the tablets upon which God sets out the Ten Commandments—but not that they could change our lives in ways that cannot be predicted and may even inaugurate for us a new life.

Certainly a religious person like Augustine, whose *Confessions* are the record of trial, error, and stumbling—not to say sin—is not a model of the modern major academic. He is too eager to display how his life reveals a pattern of blindness mixed with fleeting insight. Worst of all, he has too strong a conviction that books have a relation to life. Reading a biography of Athanasius caused him to redirect his life. Sounds a little too much like another undisciplined thinker, Montaigne. Too many now believe scholarship is only about jobs and promotions.

If we were to revitalize the humanities, we would stop insisting that they be kept in antiseptically sealed realms, and we would let the ideas and methods and materials in them wash over each other and us. During the last thirty years, as "correctness" has become the key word, the key to behavior was learning how to show others that one belonged to a definite group, such as a professional group. What markers prove I have membership in the identity group? We have abandoned learning for its own sake for the quest for credentials. This shift in values has been hard on education, which depends for its appeal on attracting people who do not know what educational institutions have to offer but hope that throwing themselves into the educational process will transform aspects of themselves. Educators have come increasingly to demonize the state of not-knowing. This is very off putting to those of us who come from homes where book learning is not a high value. Strangely, there is very little romanticizing of the role of the student—none of that "Suffer the little children to come unto me" attitude—but only the sober assessment of the economic value of having been educated. The idea that the not-yet-educated, the students, have anything to teach the teachers, as their wrestling with artworks they are confronting for the first time sets off sparks, has gone out the window. To be educated is to have a set of possessions, the keys of the tower in which a professional elite lock themselves away. So it is no surprise that the book gets emptied of content and turned into an icon of prestige. It is time for a reformation.

Scholarship and Silence

Contrast the sound of a newborn crying—the sweetest music on earth—to the cacophony and noise of men (and it's mostly men here) struggling for dominance and encouraging youngsters to publish anything, no matter, as long as it allows them to triumph over their brothers. We have been through a *Dunciad* age, a time of overproduction when sounds stop making sense. We need to get back to the most fundamental issues.

This is not a time for stopgap measures so we can "maintain our standards." Steven Greenblatt has proposed departments of English come up with funds to support graduate students buying books so they will get "hooked on books" and build little libraries of their own. Band-aids don't stop hemorrhaging. It is the time to ask what scholarship is about and—I strongly suggest—to change our standards. What we have is a system with little or no room for individual agency of the departmental members or of the books they might write. When I have delivered this essay as a lecture at different universities, I have been attacked a number of times vociferously by people who tell me I do not understand the system and that I had better "get with the program." How could I be so "retro-grade," asked one senior scholar waxing wroth in anger, trembling, face beet red, as to talk about indi-vidual responsibility in judgment?

As long as we acquiesce in this system, we will remain inside the whale. Freedom will come when we throw over the need for control, the need to be so totally in control of what can be known, and embrace ignorance. We must be willing to be fooled—mistaken in scientific and humanistic inquiry.

As we look more deeply into the problems betokened by the crisis of the monograph, I believe we have to be willing to ask the most fundamental questions. We have to ask, as scholars like Anthony Grafton and Elizabeth Eisenstein and Marshall McLuhan have helped us ask, what is the relationship between thinking, scholarship, and publication? Why do we assume—as we do—a correlation between loquaciousness and the exercise of intelligence befitting a professor?

I think we need to ponder the question of the relation between scholarship and silence. It is possible to be a great thinker and not publish anything. Heidegger pointed out that Socrates "wrote nothing." We know as scholars that sometimes we can study a body of material intently for years with a hypothesis in mind only to come up with no results, and the right thing to do then is to admit that a serious inquiry led one to conclude that there is nothing to say. Of course, Plato was there to capture what Socrates said. But much more important than noticing the contradiction between Socrates' unease with writing and the fact that he had a very high-level scribe in Plato is the case that philosophy, as we know it and think about it in the West, arose among people who felt acutely the tension between speaking and writing. This is the fault-line where friction between two different modes of intelligence proved to be just right for the emergence of philosophy.

In our scholastic rage to stuff libraries 'til they burst with publications, something got lost. And what do we do now when, increasingly, libraries do not purchase the books and books do not get read and reviewed but only counted? Here is deafening silence, but I am interested in a pregnant silence, the sort that settles in at the end of Wittgenstein's *Tractatus*. It is OK, and it might even be admirable, to produce nothing when one decides that this is appropriate. Just consider that, as Eli Friedlander writes, "the opposite of silence is not necessarily speaking with sense but, rather, making noise." Now in the academic world what we have is a cacophony, but what we should seek is the symmetry of scholars interested in reading and taking up carefully what their colleagues are producing. Some have suggested that the new possibilities for electronic publishing will alleviate our problems. In the wild ideas of some dreamers the new world of electronic publication will actually be an improvement over books. To think this way is to fail to understand that electronic publication will only make the situation worse. Moreover, it will make things worse in a way that undermines the principles behind the culture of the book. We had better put an end to such foolish talk and keep pressure on the librarians and ourselves to value the book better.

As some have imagined the electronic book it is an abdication of precisely the sort of responsibility we need to develop now and it makes impossible the act of judgment I have claimed is central to the entire process. As imagined by historian Robert Darnton, the great thing about electronic publication is that it would allow us to "dump unlimited numbers of dissertations onto the Web." The Web allows unprecedented access. This seems to me misleading, but we await results from the AHA project, for which Darnton is an advisor, to publish award-winning dissertations on-line. It is by no means clear that the Web is a good medium for words. It is fine for pornography, because like all electronic forms of reproduction it does a fine job making the gesture salient the way the hand salute performed over and over in Leni Riefenstahl's "Triumph of the Will" turns humans into mere ornaments of the will of the leader. Those who make books, by contrast, used to have to do so as individuals who stand out from the collective. Let me explain: At the heart of book making is the gathering, the tying together of materials into a package or a unity that the person or group of people pulling together are prepared to have judged. This is true whether the book is a book of sonnets written by one person or a sacred text like the Bible whose unity was the result of group decisions.

The book is a particular form made possible by the development of the codex. It is an object particularly appropriate for the library, because like a library it allows you to skim ahead or skip backwards. And it has heft. It weighs something. Its got what a dean likes in a publication: it goes bump when it hits a table. You can write on it, but at its essence is the judgment someone or some group made that it formed a unity, and it is this unity that any readers of the book are called upon to judge. Whenever we enter a new book it is with the question, what unifies the materials the author has brought together in it? The most clever books keep us guessing, which is why we love novels plotted with ingenuity where the writer holds us in suspense. Benjamin insists the written novel is different in kind from the oral tale, but I am not so sure. There is an absolute symmetry between what the book is in production and what it is in reception—a gathering—and it is this symmetry that makes for the special beauty of the book. If the life of a scholar is a calling, a vocation, it is one that is analogous to the calling a book makes to us to read it and judge it. A book is not, nor ever will be a dump. The book emerges from silence not from cacophony. The book features the highest signal to noise ratio possible of any means of communication.

I have become over the years most intrigued by the scholars who do not want to publish, who hardly even want to talk about what they know. "One should speak only where one must not be silent," wrote Nietzsche in *Human, All Too Human*. I try to listen to their hesitations, the clutch in the voice, that suggests someone is holding something back that needs to break forth. I try to be as much as possible like Sam Phillips listening to Elvis stammering into sense. Some of them are afraid to speak lest they risk ridicule. Some are timid, but not the way Fish is timid. Maybe these few might be timid or modest in the face of great questions whose complexity they truly appreciate. Some are simply appalled by all the profusion and do not wish to contribute more to the glut. They can see the truly valuable is likely to be ignored. The true innovators are the ones most likely to be beset with epistemological crises because they have wandered off to places where there are no other travelers. Such people may spend many days of their lives like explorers trying to get to one of the poles, uncertain whether they had because snow obscures the sky and makes getting a precise fix on location impossible. History provides too many examples of the truly bold thinker being resisted. Remember that even bold Picasso held back his "Desmoiselles d'Avignon" until six years after he painted it, not wanting to face the opprobrium. Gotta know when to hold'em, know when to fold'em. Timing is all.

In our moment of high scholasticism, fewer and fewer schools will tolerate this sort of independence from the increasingly rigid norms for publication. It is as if the schools were saying implicitly that in order to win tenure you have to prove that you are not an independent mind by subjecting yourself to the rules and goals of high productivity. But I think one thing to do is to put new pressure on the book by demanding that it be more substantial before it can be accepted and published. We are tired of McDonald's hamburgers. We want something that is slow cooked. I think we can put more pressure on publishers to find the important books that some of the people who don't want to break the silence could write. It really is often the best who are in no rush to write and publish. There are too many people too eager to publish, and not enough people who are biding their time and letting a project grow great within them. Some of the economists of the Rational Expectations School had the idea that there are times in economic history when it is "time to build." The same is true in the academic world. There are times when it is good to build up ideas, to play with them, and experiment with them and not rush with them to print.

I spend a lot of time among the philosophers, and I know that to a great extent they live in a different world from literary scholars. When we talk of oral cultures, one might assume they are populated by primitives. Well, I live in an oral universe as a publisher. I used to be embarrassed about this, but I'll freely admit it today. And so do the philosophers. You'll remember Derrida chastising Plato for his reluctance to enter the culture of writing. There is something about thought—that is, free thought, free speech—that resists being brought into material form. Derrida is another one of our current thinkers who seems like such a rebel, but if you were to look at his critique of Plato and "logocentrism" in the light of my argument I think it becomes plain that he promotes the biases of our age towards print and against the oral. For the sake of setting himself up as the ultimate rebel, another Last Man, he really just played upon our own prejudices in favor of publication, a prejudice I share.

By contrast, most philosophers now and over the ages have been for all practical purposes icono-clasts. A story that hit me hard was about Rogers Albritton who just before he died spent some of his precious time shredding all his lecture notes so that kind friends would not edit them and bring them to someone like me to publish. Earlier in his career his friend Donald Davidson conspired with several others

admirers of Albritton to put him in a situation where
he had to publish something: They campaigned to get
him elected the President of the Pacific Division of
the American Philosophical Association. One duty of
the President is to deliver an address at the annual
meeting. Those addresses are always published in the
proceedings, and so Albritton was tricked into
publishing.

As with Albritton, I have the strongest sense
that many of the people who have the most to say are
most reluctant to say it. And I think the academy
should enlist the publishers to try to get some of the
silent people to talk. Forget the blabbermouths. They
will find their way. Heidegger writes that "all great
Western thinkers after Socrates, with all their great-
ness, had to be fugitives." That which has not yet
reached the point of being formulated in the minds of
people flickers and teases us just beyond reach of
words until we find the words to give body to thought.
Some profound thinkers like to linger at the margins
of thought: "Heard melodies are sweet, but those
unheard/Are sweeter." The intelligent person wants to
express a thought, but first of all wants to explore it
and knows one has to be delicate. Thinking can be
like catching butterflies and not like watching a light-
ning storm. Some of the greatest thinkers hesitated
before speaking. John Rawls was a stutterer who was—
I know from trying with no luck for years—most
uneager to bring his work into print. Judgment plays a
very important role in thinking and deciding what is
fit for articulating before a public in lecture or writing.
Many brilliant souls judge their work too harshly. In

the era of scarcity that seems upon us, publishers might be newly charged to scour the world of learning in quest of those pregnant with thought whose hitherto unformulated ideas need help finding shape on paper.

Some of my greatest joys of the present moment are books that are written and done by scholars I am still shocked I managed to extract books from. I have come to understand that the reason these authors did not want to take the time to get their thoughts down on paper is because they are so impatient. Their minds are so fast they can hardly stand the slowness of conversation, but that they can manage. It's print that's the problem. Isn't that putting things too strongly? No. There is a conflict that deeply intelligent people still feel and will always feel between the authoritarianism of print and the authority one seeks by speaking and publishing. In his rush to show he is so clever, Derrida—very much Oedipus in this— misses something that Plato knows in his bones: that it was in the play or tension that the people of his time felt (uniquely in the West) between orality and literacy that Western philosophy emerged. What was Plato's objection to writing? The power to rule over us in silence because people defer to its authority. Here is a potentially lethal silence. We need to keep alive the necessity of making a judgment between the times when it is wise to be silent and when it is wise to talk (see *Phaedrus*). When we defer as when we outsource tenure decisions we betray a craven attitude to authority that does not become us. The perennial problem is that humans are always tempted to defer absolutely to masters and thereby to become slaves to others or to their own earlier thoughts as reified in writing or print; they are not challenged to become or remain the masters of their own minds as they must be when they must make up their minds and speak on the spot in dialogue with others themselves, entering the space of reason as free people.

I think our present mania for publication is a great insult to the dignity of thought, the dignity upon which the authority society might bestow on us is based. Deep thought does not always announce itself in shouts, but sometimes in whispers.

We need to reorient the humanities within the university. Departments have to tell the administrators in some nice, but forceful way, "no." They have to take back the governance of the community of scholars the way some journal editors are now seizing back their journals from rapacious publishers who want to gouge university libraries. In the humanities we have to root out an attitude of complacency in front of the system whether it comes from the administrators or from ourselves (as it does to some considerable extent). We have to be ready to explain ourselves and not find it insulting when we are asked to do so and luxuriate in the aestheticized helplessness to which we have become habituated. And we have to dare look at new things and develop new theories. Humanists have to counter the iconoclastic attitude about books and art that has come to dominate the humanities. We have to embrace art once again and show how the interaction of readers, viewers, and listeners can precipitate the sorts of experiences that allow our souls to spring forth into momentary glory. Experience is for the humanist what experiments are for the scientist, the key events we seek to explore.

If the humanities are about judgment, they are about that judgment that something is new in my interaction with some artistic objects. When we are ready to explain ourselves and when we are ready again to encounter the artwork, that is, when we set our eyes once again upon the prize of the aesthetic experience, we will find students and we will find the support we so desperately need to do our work. ■

Further Readings

Hannah Arendt, *Responsibility and Judgment*, ed. by Jerome Kohn (New York: Schocken Books, 2003).

Herbert S. Bailey, Jr., *The Rate of Publication of Scholarly Monographs in the Humanities and Social Sciences, 1978-1988* (New York: Association of American University Press, 1990).

Theodore C. Bergstrom, "Free Labor for Costly Journals?" *Journal of Economic Perspectives* 15 (2001): 183-198.

Mario Biagioli, "From Book Censorship to Academic Peer Review," *Emergences* 12 (2002): 11-45.

Paul Bové, "The Crisis of Editing," *ADE Bulletin*, no. 131 (Spring 2001), pp. 34-40.

Jessica Chalmers, "The Academic Character (With The Dictionary of Received Ideas)," Unpublished ms.

Robert Darnton, "The New Age of the Book," *New York Review of Books*, vol. 46 (18 March 1999).

Umberto Eco, "Will Books Become Obsolete?" *Al-Ahram Weekly*, 30 November 2003.

Leigh Estabrook, with Bijan Warner, "The Book as Gold Standard for Tenure and Promotion in the Humanistic Disciplines," *A Report Prepared for the December 2, 2003, meeting of Committee on Institutional Cooperation Summit on Scholarly Communication in the Humanities and Social Sciences.*

Stanley Fish, *Doing What Comes Naturally* (Durham, N.C.: Duke University Press, 1989).

Stanley Fish, *How Milton Works* (Cambridge: Harvard University Press, 2001).

Stanley Fish, *Is There a Text in This Class?* (Cambridge: Harvard University Press, 1980).

Bruno Latour and Peter Weibel, *Iconoclash: Beyond the Image Wars in Science, Religion, and Art* (Cambridge, MA: MIT Press, 2002).

Peter A. Lawrence, "The Politics of Publication: Authors, Reviewers and Editors Must Act to Protect the Quality of Research," *Nature* 422 (20 March 2003): 259-61.

John McDowell, *Mind and World* (Cambridge: Harvard University Press, 1996)

John McDowell, "Transcendental Empiricism," Unpublished ms.

Marshall McLuhan, *The Gutenberg Galaxy: The Making of Typographic Man* (Toronto: University of Toronto Press, 1962).

Joel Mokyr, *The Gifts of Athena: Historical Origins of the Knowledge Economy* (Princeton: Princeton University Press, 2002).

Talcott Parsons and Gerald M. Platt, *The American University* (Cambridge: Harvard University Press, 1973).

Richard Rorty, *Philosophy and the Mirror of Nature* (Princeton: Princeton University Press, 1979).

Michael Sandel, "What Money Can't Buy: The Moral Limits of Markets," *The Tanner Lectures of Human Values*, Balliol College, Oxford, May 11 and 12, 1998.

Lindsay Waters, "The Age of Incommensurability," *boundary 2*, vol. 28 (2001), pp 133-72.

Lindsay Waters, "A Modest Proposal for Preventing the Books of the Members of the MLA from Being a Burden to Their Authors, Publishers, or Audiences," *PMLA* vol. 115 (2000), pp. 316-17.

Lindsay Waters, "The Tyranny of the Monograph," *Chronicle of Higher Education*, 20 April 2001, pp. B7-B10.